Exploration Into INDIA

ANITA GANERI

New **Discovery** B·O·O·K·S

NEW YORK

First American publication 1994 by New Discovery Books, Macmillan Publishing Company, 866 Third Avenue, New York, NY 10022

Macmillan Publishing Company is part of the Maxwell Communication Group of Companies.

Library of Congress Cataloging-in-Publication Data

Ganeri, Anita, 1961-
  Exploration into India/Anita Ganeri
      p.   cm.
  Includes index.
  ISBN 0-02-718082-4
  1. India—Juvenile literature.   [1. India—History.]   I. Title.
DS407.G32   1994
954—dc20   93-43716

SUMMARY: An explanation of discoveries made in India, from the beginnings of time up to the 19th century explorers, with a postscript about modern India.

First published in Great Britain in 1994 by Belitha Press Limited, 31 Newington Green, London N16 9PU

Printed in Hong Kong for Imago

Previous page: **A**mber *Fort, Jaipur, Rajasthan.*

This page: **A** *nineteenth century engraving of the royal tombs of Golconda (see page 34).*

Photographic credits

The Ancient Art and Architecture Collection 9 bottom, 11 top, 35 right; Archiv fur Kunst und Geschichte, Berlin 27 bottom, 38 top; The Bridgeman Art Library 5, 9 top, 20, 28 bottom left by Courtesy of the Board of Trustees of the V & A and top right, 29 top left Bodleian Library, 30 top right and bottom left, 34 bottom; C M Dixon 15 top; E.T. Archive 32 bottom, 41 bottom; Mary Evans Picture Library 19 bottom, 23, 26 right, 30 top left, 31 top right, 34 top, 39 top left, 40 top left; Giraudon/The Bridgeman Art Library 22, Sonia Halliday Photographs 19 top, 21 right; Hansmann 11 bottom; Robert Harding Picture Library cover background, 7 middle and bottom, 8, 10, 13 bottom, 14, 15 bottom, 17, 21 left, 22/23 Bodleian Library, 25 bottom, 26 left British Museum, 29 top right Freer Gallery of Art, Washington, 32 top, 35 left Bibliotheque Nationale, 39 bottom left; Hulton Deutsch Collection Limited 36 right, 37 top left and bottom, 40 top right, 42 top, 43 top right; The Hutchison Library 3, 44 top right; Vanessa Kelly cover foreground, 30 middle right, 31 top left and bottom right, 38 bottom, 39 top right, 44 bottom center left, bottom left and bottom right, 45 left; The Mansell Collection 2, 7 top, 36 bottom middle, 41 top; The National Trust Photographic Library 36 bottom left; Andrew Oliver title page, 27 top, 28 top left and top middle, 28/29, 31 bottom left 44 top center left and center right, 45 right, back cover; Popperfoto 42 bottom, 43 bottom; Royal Geographical Society Picture Library 25 top, 39 bottom right, 40 bottom; Syndication International 12, 13 top, 33 top Pierpoint Morgan Library and bottom; Rijksmuseum, Amsterdam 37 top right; India Office Library 43 top left.

Editor: Jill Laidlaw
Designer: Andrew Oliver
Picture researcher: Vanessa Kelly
Series consultant: Shane Winser, Royal Geographical Society, London
Consultants: Professor David Arnold of the School of Oriental and African Studies, London

Contents

1 Exploring India
The Story of India   5
The Indus Valley Civilization   6
The Aryans Arrive   8
The Greeks in India   10

2 India to A.D. 1001
Reforms and New Religions   12
The Glory of the Guptas   14
Chinese Explorers   16
Early Traders   18

3 India under the Muslims
Muslim Invaders and Explorers   20
Travelers' Tales   22
South India through the Eyes of
   Travelers   24
The Mogul Empire   26

4 The European Presence in India
European Traders   32
European Travelers   34

5 The British Raj 1756–1947
Explorers and Rulers   36
Princes and Politics   38
Life in the Raj   40

6 Modern India
Toward Independence   42
India Today   44

Time Chart   46
Glossary   47
Index   48

A *priest from the Toda tribe, who live in the Nilgiri Hills in South India*

CHINA

KASHMIR

HINDU KUSH

AFGHANISTAN   • Khyber Pass   • Islamabad

HIMALAYAS

NEPAL

▲ Mount Everest

BHUTAN

SIKKIM

• Harappa

Sutlej River

IRAN

PUNJAB PLAINS

Ganges River

• Meerut

Delhi •

• Lucknow

BANGLADESH

Indus River

• Bikaner

• Agra

• Kanpur

• Patna

Ganges River

• Jaipur

Fatehpur Sikri

Sarnath

• Mohenjo-Daro

• Jodhpur

Jamuna River

• Benares

PAKISTAN

THAR
DESERT

Bhatpara

Calcutta •

• Karachi

VINDHYA RANGE

• Sanchi

Cuttack

• Ahmadabad

Narmada River

I N D I A

India is made up of
four main geographical
regions—the mighty
Himalayas, the Indo-
Gangetic Plain, the
Deccan Plateau, and the
Thar Desert (see map).
Mount Everest, the
world's highest
mountain at 29,028
feet, is part of the
Himalayas. It stands on
the border between
Tibet and Nepal.

• Somnath

Ajanta Caves
•

GULF OF CAMBAY

EASTERN GHATS

BAY OF
BENGAL

Bombay •

DECCAN PLATEAU

Godavari River

ARABIAN

SEA

Golconda
•

• Hyderabad

WESTERN GHATS

Krishna River

GOA

India's borders have changed
many times, reflecting its
changing political situation. In
the past, India included parts of
Afghanistan, Burma, Nepal,
Pakistan, and Bangladesh. These
are now independent countries.
For the majority of this book,
however, they count as part of
India. Pakistan and Bangladesh
split from India in 1947 as West
and East Pakistan. East Pakistan
became independent Bangladesh
in 1971.

• Vijayanagar

Madras •

Mysore •

Pondicherry •

India has three seasons,
dictated by the
movement of the rain-
bearing **monsoon**
winds. The hot season
begins in February, the
wet monsoon season in
June, and the cool
season in October.
Cherrapunji, in north-
east India, holds the
world record for the
most rain in a month—
30.5 feet—and in a
year—87 feet.

MALABAR COAST

Calicut •

NILGIRI HILLS

Cauvery River

Cochin •

• Madurai

INDIAN OCEAN

SRI
LANKA

CAPE COMORIN

Colombo •

1 Exploring India

The Story of India

What comes to mind when you think of India? The beautiful Taj Mahal (see page 31)? Huge elephants, ferocious tigers, shimmering peacocks, and agile monkeys? Exotic plants like **banyan** trees and mangroves? Cool cotton and spicy food? India is all these things and many others. Its sights, smells, sounds, wealth, and poverty have fascinated visitors and explorers for thousands of years. The history of India's exploration is also a history of trading and invasion—from the Aryans (see pages 8–9) to the Moguls (see pages 26–31) to the British (see pages 36–41). Each power left its mark, adding to India's diversity.

Exploring People of Yesterday and Today

Very little is known about the first inhabitants of India. It is thought that 200,000 to 400,000 years ago there were two distinct groups of peoples who spoke different languages and used tools made of either solid stone or flakes of stone. This indistinct period gave way to the great Indus Valley civilization (3000 B.C.), which lasted for 4,000 years. Many different types, tribes, and groups of people live in India today. Several of these peoples, such as the Nagas of the northeastern hill tracts, have their own homelands within India.

Exploring This Book

This book is divided into six chapters. After this chapter on ancient India, there is a chapter that covers the Muslim invasion up until A.D. 1001. Chapter 3 looks at India under Muslim rule, while chapter 4 deals with the arrival of the first European travelers and traders. Chapter 5 explores India under British rule, with the final chapter looking at India today.

Vishnu the preserver, one of the major gods of the Hindu religion. Here he visits the earth in the guise of a fish, to save mankind.

Religion in India

Three-quarters of all Indians are Hindus. They believe in a supreme being, called Brahman, whose various characters are represented by three main gods—Brahma (the creator), Vishnu (the preserver), and Shiva (the destroyer). There are thousands of other gods and goddesses. Some people worship in temples, others in small shrines at home. But Hinduism is an extremely flexible religion—some Hindus do not perform any formal worship. Hindus believe in **reincarnation**. For them, the ultimate goal is moksha, or salvation from the cycle of birth and rebirth.

Other major Indian religions include Islam (see page 19), Buddhism (see page 13), and Sikhism (see page 35).

The Indus Valley Civilization

The first, and greatest, civilization in ancient India developed around the valley of the Indus River (now in Pakistan) in about 3000 B.C. By 2500 B.C., it had reached the height of its power. The Indus Valley civilization was larger than any other ancient empire, including those of Egypt and **Mesopotamia**. Its two great centers were the cities of Mohenjo Daro and Harappa.

An artist's reconstruction of the city of Mohenjo Daro

City Planning

The Indus cities were built along careful plans. A city was divided into two parts—the lower town, where most people lived, and a fortified **citadel**, built on a raised brick platform. The streets of the lower town were laid out in a grid pattern, with wide main roads intersected by narrower side streets. Houses were built of mud bricks and many had courtyards. Each house had a bathroom and an efficient drainage system. The citadel was protected by a massive brick wall. It is thought to have been the city's religious and administrative center. In Mohenjo Daro, the citadel also housed the Great Bath (see 1), used for religious rituals. Each city also had huge granaries (see 2) for storing precious supplies of grain.

Indus Life

The Indus Valley civilization had highly organized systems of trade and transportation, with the cities as centers of commerce. Trade was based on agricultural produce, grown on the fertile river plains. The main crops were wheat, barley, dates, and melons. People worked as farmers, merchants, potters, bead makers, metalworkers, and so on. Many pottery figures have been found at the Indus sites. Some show gods and goddesses. Others are toys, such as bird-shaped whistles and cows with nodding heads. The Indus people loved jewelry and used tiny pottery animals as beads.

The Indus in Decline

In 2000 B.C., the Indus Valley civilization collapsed. No one is sure why this happened. The cities may have been destroyed by frequent, terrible floods or by the river changing course and causing the farmland to dry up. Another theory is that the Indus people overgrazed the land, leading to smaller harvests and a decrease in trade.

Sir Alexander Cunningham

Exploring the Past

Most of our knowledge of the Indus Valley civilization and of ancient India comes from archaeological finds. In the 19th century, the British **archaeologist**, Sir Alexander Cunningham explored and **excavated** many ancient sites. He visited Harappa in 1853 and 1873. But the first real excavation of the Indus cities was begun in the 1920s and 1930s by the Archaeological Survey of India, under another British archaeologist, Sir John Marshall. Marshall and his assistant R. D. Banerji found two previously unknown Indus sites dating back to the third millennium B.C.

*Among the most interesting **artifacts** found at the Indus sites are small carved stone seals. These were used by merchants to seal bundles of goods. Many of the seals show animals, such as one-horned bulls, elephants, and tigers. Some show religious scenes. Each seal also had an inscription, proving that the Indus Valley civilization had its own form of writing. Unfortunately, no one has yet been able to understand it.*

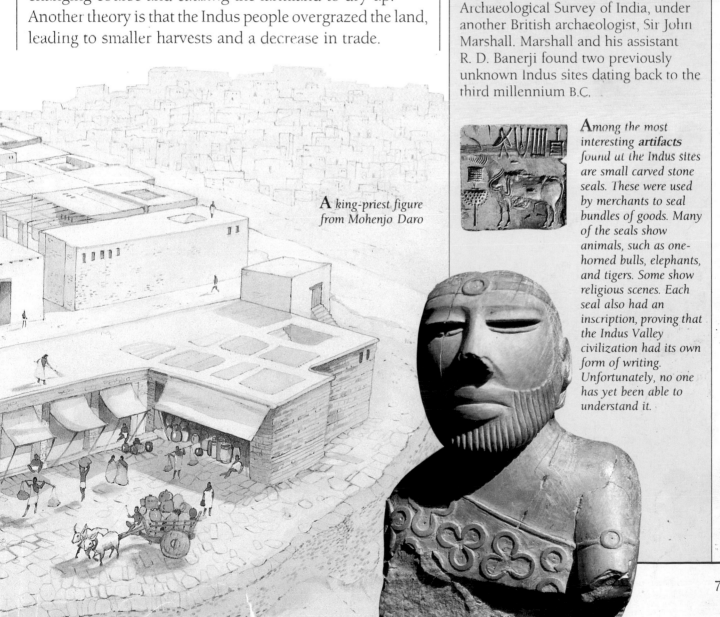

A king-priest figure from Mohenjo Daro

The Aryans Arrive

From their arrival in India in about 1500 B.C., the Aryans spread southeast through the Indus Valley and down into the Ganges Valley.

The 16 states of Aryan India in the sixth century B.C.

The foothills of the Hindu Kush Mountains to the northwest of India, which now lie in modern-day Pakistan and Afghanistan

In about 1500 B.C., groups of **Indo-Europeans** traveled from Iran to northwest India. They called themselves Aryans. They spread through the Indus Valley, then moved eastward toward the Ganges Valley. The early Aryans roamed from place to place, searching out pasture for their herds of cattle. Gradually, they became more settled and formed themselves into small villages, which grew into towns as the Aryans began to farm and develop their trading activities. The time of the Aryans is called the Vedic age.

The Aryans Explore

The Aryans were divided into various independent tribes, ruled by chiefs called rajas and by two councils—the sabha and the samiti. The tribes gradually expanded their territories and began to trade, **bartering** for goods with cows and gold. With trade came increased prosperity. There were many conflicts among the tribes as they jostled for power. One famous battle, called the Battle of the Ten Kings, saw the victory of the Bharata tribe over an alliance of ten rival tribes. The modern name for India, Bharat, which is **Sanskrit** for "India," comes from this tribe. The famous Aryan epic, *Mahabharata*, is the story of many cousins and their endless battles.

By the sixth century B.C., the tribes had grown into small kingdoms and **republics**, and the center of Aryan power had moved to the Ganges Valley. The rulers of the 16 most powerful states—the mahajanapadas—struggled for control of the region. The kingdom of Magadha emerged as the victor. It controlled the valley and the main trade routes along the Ganges River for several centuries.

Indra, *the Aryan god of war and the sky, mounted on his white battle elephant*

Aryan Religion

The Aryans worshiped many gods, especially those connected with nature and the world around them. Their most important god was Indra, god of the sky, rain, thunder, and war. Other major gods included Varuna, controller of the universe, Surya, the sun god, Agni, the god of fire, and Yama, the god of death. The Aryans offered sacrifices, often of animals, to the gods to gain their blessings. The priests who conducted the sacrifices and rituals were among the most important members of Aryan society. The offerings were placed in a sacred fire that carried them to the gods.

The mingling of ideas from the Aryan and Indus Valley religions formed the basis of Hinduism (see page 5).

The Rig-Veda

One of our main sources of information about Aryan religion is a collection of 1,028 hymns called the *Rig-Veda*. These hymns were recited by the priests at sacrifices and ceremonies. Some hymns were addressed to specific gods. There were also battle hymns, observations, and **dialogues**. The Aryans spoke Sanskrit and passed the hymns down by word of mouth. A hymn had to be spoken and pronounced perfectly for it to be effective. It was not until centuries later that the hymns were written down for the first time. The *Rig-Veda* remains one of the most sacred Hindu holy texts and its hymns are still sung at weddings and funerals.

The Caste System

The class a person belonged to became important during Aryan times and these classes formed the basis of the caste system that still continues in India today. The three highest classes were the priests, called Brahmins, warriors and nobles, called Kshatriyas, and merchants, called Vaisyas. A fourth class, Sudras, was made up of the non-Aryan people who originally lived in the areas invaded by the Aryans. Sudras were usually farmers. The *Rig-Veda* contains an account of how the caste system was created from a cosmic being, Purusa. The Brahmins came from his mouth, the Kshatriyas from his arms, the Vaisyas from his thighs, and the Sudras from his feet.

Agni, *the Aryan god of fire. The sacred fire was central to many Aryan religious ceremonies and rituals. It was thought that it linked heaven and earth, carrying people's sacrifices up to the gods.*

9

The Greeks in India

During the sixth century B.C., the Persians (see map) moved into northwest India. The region of Gandhara became a part of the Persian Empire. A Greek doctor, Ktesias, who lived at the Persian court in the fifth century B.C., left an interesting, if inaccurate, account of life in northwest India. In it he describes a tiger as having three rows of teeth in each jaw and a sting at the tip of its tail, which it shot at its enemy like an arrow!

Alexander and India

In 327 B.C., however, the Persians were overthrown by Alexander the Great of Macedon. Alexander came to the throne of Macedon, in northeastern Greece, in 336 B.C., when he was just 20 years old. Within 13 years he had conquered a vast empire that stretched from Greece through Egypt and Persia to India.

By 330 B.C., Alexander had defeated the Persians and their emperor, Darius. He now set out to reach the easternmost part of Darius's empire—in India. He fought his way through Bactria (see map), crossed the Hindu Kush (see map), and reached the Indus River in 326 B.C. At the battle of Hydaspes, he defeated the Punjabi king Porus and his troop of 200 battle elephants. Alexander was so impressed by Porus's dignity and courage that he left him in charge of the Punjab. So far, the Indian campaign had been a success. But, on reaching the Beas River (see map), Alexander's army refused to go farther and he was forced to turn back.

The map above shows Alexander's empire at its greatest extent.

Alexander's defeat of the Persians paved the way for his journey into India.

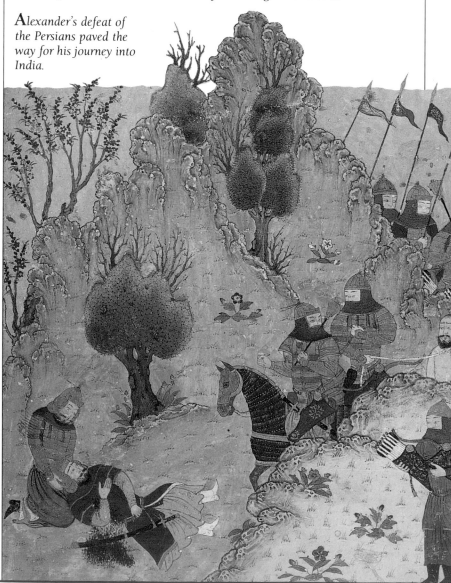

The Search for the "Ocean"

Alexander had heard many tales of India. Many Greek writers had portrayed India as a place of monsters, poisons, gold, and gems. Reports had reached Greece of giant gold-digging ants, wool growing on trees, men who lay on their backs and used their huge feet to shade them from the sun, and elephants that could be trained to sew.

Alexander wanted to solve the mystery of the "Ocean." He had been taught that this was a huge, continuous sea that flowed in a circle around the land. He believed that if he crossed the Indus River, he would find the "Ocean." When he finally reached the Indian Ocean, he sacrificed some bulls to the Greek sea-god, Poseidon, for leading him to his goal.

Alexander's quest to find the "Ocean" was fueled by fabulous, largely untrue, Greek accounts of India.

The Art of Gandhara

A lasting reminder of the Greeks in India is the influence of their artistic style on Indian art and sculpture. This was very strongly felt in Gandhara in the first and second centuries A.D. Greek and Buddhist (see page 13) styles of sculpture merged to produce graceful statues, draped in long, flowing robes. This was not the result of Alexander's legacy, however. Greek styles of art were copied by the Romans, whose traders were in regular contact with India (see page 18).

A *head of the Buddha from Gandhara from the first century* A.D.

The capital of the Mauryan Empire

The Rise of Chandragupta Maurya

In about 321 B.C., a young prince, Chandragupta Maurya, seized power and founded the great Mauryan Empire. He built his capital at Pataliputra (modern-day Patna). He defeated the Seleucid Greeks, who had inherited the eastern part of Alexander's empire, but remained on friendly terms with them. In about 305 B.C., the Seleucids sent an **envoy**, Megasthenes, to Chandragupta's court at Pataliputra. Megasthenes wrote a detailed account of his Indian experiences in a book called the *Indika*.

Megasthenes's book was important because it formed the Christian view of India right up until the Middle Ages (c.500–c.1500). In the *Indika*, Megasthenes describes the empire's administration, economy, and secret service. Megasthenes also relates how Chandragupta lived in great luxury at Pataliputra, in a huge wooden palace. The Greek reports that Chandragupta lived in fear of his life and slept in a different bedroom every night to avoid being assassinated. Whenever he left the palace, he was guarded by a band of women on horseback. Chandragupta died about 297 B.C.

11

Reforms and New Religions

The empire of King Asoka Maurya

A fragment of one of Asoka's rock edicts

Under Asoka, the grandson of Chandragupta, the Mauryan Empire reached the height of its power. Asoka came to the throne in 269 B.C. and became the greatest ruler of ancient India. Because of his powerful personality, most of India came under Mauryan rule.

The Kalinga Campaign

One of the few places in India that had resisted the Mauryans was Kalinga on the east coast (in modern-day Orissa). In 260 B.C., Asoka launched a successful but ferocious campaign against Kalinga. According to Asoka, 100,000 people were killed in battle, many more died after, and 150,000 were **deported**. Asoka was filled with remorse. In an effort to make amends, he converted to the Buddhist religion, which preaches nonviolence (see box).

Asoka's Edicts

Our main source of information about Asoka and his reign is the collection of edicts (laws) and inscriptions that he had carved on rocks and sandstone pillars throughout his empire. These were deciphered for the first time in 1837 by a British **orientalist**, James Prinsep. Some were placed at the borders of the empire, showing its huge size. Others were located in places connected with the Buddha or along **pilgrimage** routes. The inscriptions begin with the words, "The King, The Beloved of the Gods, Piyadassi, speaks thus..." Some are accounts of Asoka's conversion to Buddhism. Others are **proclamations** from Asoka to the people. They explain his policy of dharma, which stressed tolerance, respect for other people, social responsibility, and nonviolence. Special officers were appointed to travel throughout the land and explain dharma.

Thanks to the edicts, we now have a good picture of Asoka's personality and reign. Before they were deciphered, very little was known about this great king.

Asoka Explores His Kingdom

Asoka traveled widely through the empire listening to people's opinions. This was highly unusual at a time when emperors were only really seen outside their palaces to go hunting or to go into battle. Asoka tried to make people's lives easier by building roads and rest houses, setting up free hospitals and veterinary clinics, bathing tanks, and drinking places for cattle, and planting shady trees.

*A*soka's famous Lion Capital can be seen on India's modern-day banknotes.

The Sarnath Lion Capital

The four-lion capital (sculpture on top of a column), which is a symbol of the modern republic of India, originally stood on top of one of Asoka's finest pillars. It stood in the deer park at Sarnath, near Benares, where the Buddha preached his first sermon (called the Turning of the Wheel of Law). The four lions look in four directions, so that their roars reach the four corners of the earth just as the Buddha's teachings do. Below them are four royal animals—the horse, bull, lion, and elephant—and four wheels, representing the Buddha's teachings. The lions originally supported a huge wheel, the symbol of Buddhism.

*T*his statue of the Buddha preaching at Sarnath dates from A.D. 318 to 566.

The Teachings of the Buddha

The Buddha, or "**Enlightened** One," was born in about 560 B.C. His real name was Siddhartha Gautama and he was the son of a king. Siddhartha lived in the royal palace, surrounded by luxury. But he became more and more dissatisfied with life and, at the age of 29, decided to give up all his belongings, leave the palace, and roam the world in search of truth. He found that the best path to follow to the truth was one of meditation, non-violence, and moderation, and these elements form the basis of his teachings. The Buddha wandered throughout India for 44 years, preaching his message. Buddhism had great appeal for ordinary people. It had no caste system (see box on page 9), so they did not feel downtrodden, and the Buddha preached in the popular, local language, rather than Sanskrit, the language of the upper castes.

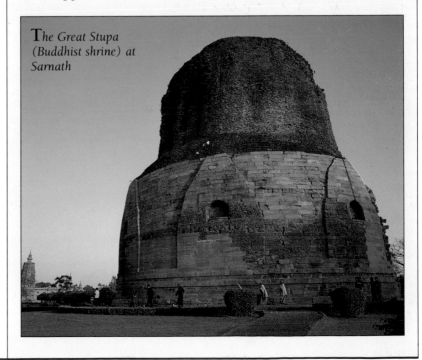

*T*he Great Stupa (Buddhist shrine) at Sarnath

The Glory of the Guptas

This map shows the probable extent of the Gupta Empire under King Chandra Gupta II.

Shiva the destroyer, one of the three major gods of Hinduism

A carving of Vishnu sleeping on the coils of the many-headed serpent Ananta. It comes from one of the earliest known Gupta temples in central India and dates from about A.D. 425.

Asoka died in 231 B.C. and the Mauryan Empire began to break up and finally collapsed in 184 B.C. For the next 500 years, India was split into a number of small kingdoms and republics. Then, in about A.D. 320, the second great Indian empire emerged in the Ganges Valley and Magadha—that of the Guptas. The first Gupta king, Chandra Gupta I, established himself by marrying into a respected royal family. Chandra Gupta I was succeeded by his son, Samudra Gupta. He was an active military campaigner, extending the empire during the 40 years of his reign. In about A.D. 380, Samudra was succeeded by his son, Chandra Gupta II, the greatest of the Gupta kings.

The Golden Age

The time of the Gupta Empire (c. A.D. 320–550) is often called the classical age of India. Under the **patronage** of the Guptas, literature, art, architecture, and science flourished. Hinduism became the major religion of the empire, rather than Buddhism. Many temples were built with donations from wealthy families. Colleges were established for religious and formal education. Trade brought continuing prosperity. Textile making was one of the most important industries of the time, and large quantities of silk, cotton, **muslin**, and linen were produced for export.

The classical age reached its peak during the reign of Chandra Gupta II (A.D. 380–415). The great Sanskrit poet Kalidasa is thought to have lived and written his poems and plays at Chandra Gupta's court. Kalidasa was described as one of the "nine gems" of the court. Sanskrit was encouraged as the language of the court and of the aristocracy. In the plays of the time, upper-class characters spoke Sanskrit, while lower-class characters and all women spoke Prakrit, the common language!

T*he direction of the Hun invasion*

The Hun Invasion

Chandra Gupta II was succeeded in A.D. 415 by his son, Kumara Gupta. During his reign (A.D. 415–455), the empire was threatened in the northwest by a central Asian tribe called the Huns. Under the later Gupta kings, the empire gradually grew weaker as the Hun invasions became stronger. By the end of the sixth century, it had broken up into several smaller kingdoms.

Achievements in Science

Indian science and mathematics were highly advanced by the time of the Guptas. A decimal system was already in use. Indian numerals later reached Europe via the Arabs and replaced Roman numerals. We still use them today. In the second century A.D., the oldest surviving Indian medical textbook was written. It was also a time of great discoveries in Indian astronomy. In about A.D. 499, the astronomer Aryabhata proposed that the earth was a sphere and spun on its axis. He also calculated the length of a year extremely accurately as 365.3586 days. At the time, his theories were rejected as being too revolutionary.

The Ajanta Paintings

T*he finest examples of Indian art from the classical period are the paintings inside the Buddhist cave temples of Ajanta in West India. The caves were cut from solid rock, from about the second century onward, but the paintings date from Gupta times. Only fragments from this period remain on the cave walls, mainly showing scenes from the life of Buddha. The artists prepared the rock surface with a coating of clay mixed with cow dung, straw, and hair, covered with a smooth layer of white plaster. The painting was done while the wall was still damp. The caves were abandoned in the eighth century. They were rediscovered in the 19th century by British soldiers out hunting tigers. In the early 1920s, two Italian art experts began the task of restoring the paintings, which had decayed because of pollution.*

Chinese Explorers

Despite the **revival** of Hinduism during the Gupta period, Buddhism was still a major force in India. Buddhist **missionaries** from India traveled far and wide, spreading the word of the Buddha. In about A.D. 100, Buddhism reached China. Chinese Buddhist monks wanted to learn more about their religion and their holy books, and to visit the places where the Buddha had lived and taught.

The Journey of Fa-Hsien

Fa-Hsien was born in China in about A.D. 370. He became a Buddhist monk and decided to travel to India to bring back Buddhist texts, which he later translated from Sanskrit into Chinese. He set off on his journey in 399. To reach India, Fa-Hsien had to cross the dreaded Takla Makan Desert (see map), following a trail of dead men's bones, avoiding bandits, and battling against the cold and his own tiredness. Then he crossed the Pamir Mountains and on through the Hindu Kush (see map). He described the mountains as sheltering "dragons which, if once provoked, spit out their poison." Once he reached India, Fa-Hsien stayed at many Buddhist monasteries to study and debate with the monks. He also visited the Buddha's birthplace in Kapilavastu, the site of his enlightenment in Bodh Gaya, and the site of his first sermon in Sarnath (see page 13). When he returned to China 15 years later, Fa-Hsien wrote a detailed account of his travels in his book, *The Memoirs of the Buddha's Dominions.*

Fa-Hsien and Chandra Gupta II

Fa-Hsien traveled around India during the reign of Chandra Gupta II. He reports that the empire was peaceful and prosperous. There was little crime and he was able to travel across India without running into any trouble. He does not give many details about the ruler himself but says that the administration seemed mild and just. Fa-Hsien also noted that most "respectable" people in India were vegetarians.

*H*suan Tsang loses his way in the desert and is attacked by wild tribesmen, but eventually comes to Ha-mi.

Turfan

Hami

An-hsi

*F*a-Hsien eventually returns to China after fifteen years, laden with religious objects and manuscripts.

Huang He River

Tsingtao

*H*suan Tsang sets out for India.

Wuwei

The Journey of Hsuan Tsang

Lo-yang

TAKLA MAKAN DESERT

*F*a-Hsien crosses the Takla Makan Desert, following a trail of dead men's bones.

The Journey of Fa Hsien

Sian

Nanking River

SHAN

CHINA

*F*a-Hsien begins his journey in A.D. 399.

Yangtze

*H*suan Tsang stays at the Buddhist monastery of Nalanda

Calcutta

*F*a-Hsien sails south to Sri Lanka.

BAY OF BENGAL

*H*suan Tsang found India a less peaceful place than Fa-Hsien had. He was robbed by bandits twice and almost sacrificed to the goddess **Durga** by a band of robbers as he sailed down the Ganges River.

*F*a-Hsien returns to China, stopping in Malaysia and Indonesia on the way.

The Journey of Hsuan Tsang

More than 200 years later, in about 630, another Buddhist monk, Hsuan Tsang, set off from China to India. He had to leave China in secret, having been refused a travel permit by the emperor. His local guide abandoned him and he was forced to cross the desert alone on horseback. On the way, he was shot at by archers and lost both his water bag and his way. Things improved once he reached India. Hsuan Tsang visited many Buddhist sites and worshiped the **relics** of the Buddha. He also spent time at the great Buddhist monastery of Nalanda, where he studied Sanskrit, philosophy, and the Buddhist holy texts. Hsuan Tsang returned to China in 645 to a hero's welcome. The story goes that he needed 20 horses to carry back all the Buddhist manuscripts and statues he had collected. He spent the rest of his life translating the texts and writing his *Memoirs on Western Countries*.

Hsuan Tsang and Harsha

When Hsuan Tsang visited North India, it was mostly ruled by a king named Harsha. Hsuan Tsang greatly admired the king and spent a happy time at his court. He describes Harsha as being talented, generous, patient, and energetic. Harsha traveled constantly around his kingdom, listening to people's comments and complaints. He also loved literature and even wrote three plays himself.

The map above shows the routes followed by early traders, overland and by sea, to India.

Early traders were dazzled by the variety and quality of goods they found in India and by the colorful hustle and bustle of Indian life.

Early Traders

It was not just pilgrims and invaders who traveled to and from ancient India. From very early on, traders' routes carried the fabulous goods of India to the West via the Middle East, the Mediterranean, China, and Southeast Asia. Goods were carried both overland and by sea. India's spices, cotton, silk, and precious stones were in great demand. The merchants of India enjoyed great wealth and became highly organized through guilds, called *shreni*.

Trade with Rome

During the first century A.D., Indian trade with the mighty Roman Empire flourished. Wealthy Romans developed a taste for Indian spices and cloth. Live animals and birds were also in demand for the Roman emperors' wildbeast shows. Thousands of tigers, lions, and elephants were exported from India to Rome, together with peacocks and parrots as pets. The Romans paid for these goods in gold. Roman coins have been found all over India, especially in the south near the main trading stations. There are also lists of Indian ports in a document called the *Periplus Maris Erythraei* (*Periplus of the Erythraeum Sea*), which is thought to have been written in the first century A.D. The *Periplus* also lists India's major exports—pearls, ivory, silk, pepper, textiles, precious stones, and **tortoiseshell**.

A *traditional Arab ship carrying merchants on a trading mission*

Sea Trade and the Arabs

Arab merchants had traded with India for hundreds of years before the Romans. The discovery of the monsoon winds in the first century B.C. meant that ships could take a direct route across the Arabian Sea to the Persian Gulf and the Red Sea rather than following the slower route along the coast. One of the most important ports for the spice trade with both the Arabs and Romans was Malabar on the west coast. The decline of the Roman Empire in the fourth century A.D. gave a boost to Arab trade with India and they were soon in control of the main trading routes. The Arabs traded for horses, foodstuffs, and metals. They also learned and exported Indian rice and sugarcane growing techniques.

Sailors of all centuries have used the monsoon winds to guide them. The winds could be very treacherous.

Regions and Cultures

In the late sixth century, India split into independent kingdoms and states, each with its own distinctive identity, culture, and language. Sanskrit was still used, but for courtly and official purposes rather than everyday speech and popular literature. Instead, local languages such as Tamil, Gujarati, Bengali, and Marathi grew in importance.

The Spread of Islam

The religion of Islam was founded in Arabia in A.D. 622 by the Prophet Muhammad. It quickly spread throughout Arabia and North Africa. In 711, the Arabs conquered Sind, the region around the Indus **Delta**, and brought Islam to India. Today, more than a tenth of Indians are Muslims. There have been violent clashes between the Hindu and Muslim communities in modern-day India. But the arrival of Islam in India was peaceful. The Muslims did not try to convert people by force but gave Hindus special status as a protected people.

3 India under the Muslims

Muslim Invaders and Explorers

Mahmud of Ghazni

Although the Arabs had conquered Sind in the eighth century, the first real Muslim invasion of India began in 1001. The Turk Mahmud of Ghazni led bands of raiders from Afghanistan into northwest India almost yearly for the next 25 years. His aim was to plunder the wealth of the Hindu temples. He stole huge amounts of money, jewelry, and gold and ruthlessly destroyed many temples in the name of Islam. In 1024, he attacked the temple town of Somnath in Gujarat. The temple contained an image that was worshiped by "a thousand Brahmins continuously and washed every night in the River Ganges." Mahmud ordered the image to be smashed and its coverings of jewels, gold, and embroidered cloth to be carried back to Afghanistan.

The Delhi Sultanate

Mahmud of Ghazni died in 1030 and his place was taken by another group of Turks, under their leader, Muhammad of Ghur. By 1185, the Ghurids had control of northwest India. In 1193, they conquered Delhi, which became their headquarters. Muhammad of Ghur was assassinated in 1206 and his general, Qutb ud-Din Aibak became the first sultan of Delhi.

Timur invaded and sacked the city of Delhi in 1398, dealing a bitter blow to the Delhi Sultanate (above).

Timur's raids were bloody affairs (left).

A European engraving of Timur of 1826

Within 20 years, the sultanate had most of the Ganges Valley under its control. Aibak was a former slave and the founder of the so-called Slave Dynasty. Aibak was succeeded by Iltutmish, who ruled from 1211–1236 (see box). By 1236, the Delhi Sultanate was firmly established as the greatest power in northern India.

Dynasties and Decline

The sultanate had 35 rulers from several different dynasties from its beginnings to its decline in the 16th century. From the end of the 14th century, however, the sultanate began to decline. Territory was lost and there were arguments about who should rule. Some Muslim nobles and Hindu chiefs broke away and declared their independence. In 1398, the sultanate was attacked by the central Asian chieftain Timur. This weakened it further and it gradually shrank in size and importance. In 1526, at the battle of Panipat, the last Delhi sultan, Ibrahim, was defeated by a descendant of Timur, called Babur, who was ruler of Kabul in Afghanistan. The Mogul Empire had begun (see pages 26–31).

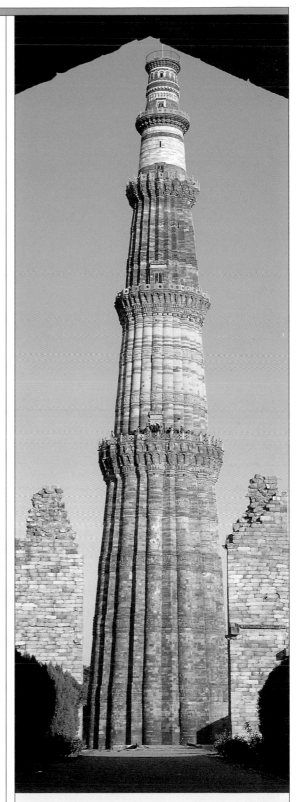

The Qutb Minar (above) near Delhi is a tall victory tower built by Qutb ud-Din Aibak in 1193. It was constructed to celebrate the first Muslim victories over the Hindus, which marked the start of the Delhi Sultanate. The tower is over 230 feet high. It has five tiers made of sandstone and marble, each with a balcony. Qutb ud-Din only saw the tower reach its first floor; the rest was completed by his successors.

Raziya Sultana

One of the most extraordinary rulers of Delhi was Raziya, the daughter of Iltutmish. Her father was a wise, tolerant leader who groomed his daughter to succeed him. Raziya reigned for a short time, from 1236 to 1240, as the first woman ruler in the Muslim world. But many of the sultanate's advisers and nobles resented having a woman on the throne and plotted her downfall and murder. She was, however, a firm and capable ruler. A historian of the time wrote that she was "wise, just, and generous," and "endowed with all the qualities befitting a king!"

Travelers' Tales

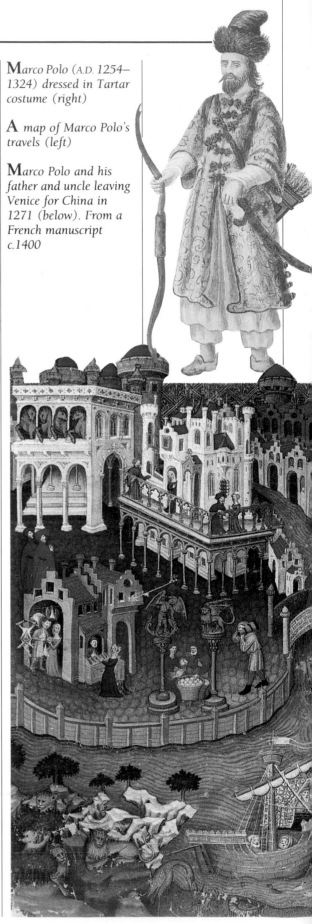

Marco Polo (A.D. 1254–1324) dressed in Tartar costume (right)

A map of Marco Polo's travels (left)

Marco Polo and his father and uncle leaving Venice for China in 1271 (below). From a French manuscript c.1400

Apart from the Muslims, there were other foreign visitors to India during the 13th and 14th centuries. Their eyewitness accounts of events have been extremely valuable in piecing together a picture of Indian life during the early part of the Muslims' rule. Two of the most famous of these travelers were the Italian Marco Polo and the Moroccan Ibn Battuta.

Marco Polo

Marco Polo was born in 1254 in Venice, Italy. At that time, Venice was a great commercial center. Marco's family were wealthy merchants and made several journeys to the Middle East and Asia in search of trading opportunities. In 1271, Marco joined his father and uncle on their travels. They traveled overland, with the court of the great **Kublai Khan** in China as their final destination. Their journey took them through Turkey, Persia, and Afghanistan, crossing into India through the Hindu Kush to join the **Old Silk Road**. The Polos spent 17 years in China. On their return journey to Venice, Marco traveled up the west and east coasts of India and visited Tamil Nadu in southern India. In his book, *The Travels of Marco Polo,* he comments on the thriving trade in horses brought from Arabia.

Marco Polo died in 1324 after an adventurous life that inspired many explorers such as Christopher Columbus.

Early Europeans

During the 15th and 16th centuries, another group of people began to arrive in India. They were Europeans who came to trade rather than to travel. They had heard stories of the great wealth of the East and were unhappy that the Arabs were controlling its trade and its profits. To take advantage, the Europeans needed to cut out the Arab **middlemen** and trade directly with Asia. The first European country to make its mark on India was Portugal. By the end of the 15th century, the Portuguese had found a direct sea route to India and established trading posts on the west coast, of which Goa was the most important (see pages 32–33).

Ibn Battuta, the Traveler of Islam, traveled 74,000 miles in his lifetime.

Ibn Battuta

Ibn Battuta, known as the Traveler of Islam, was born in Tangier, Morocco, in 1304. In 1325, at the age of 21, he left Morocco on a pilgrimage to Mecca, the holy city of the Muslims. This was the start of a life of traveling in which he covered an amazing 74,000 miles and visited almost every Muslim country, together with Southeast Asia and China. His only rule was never to travel the same road twice. In 1332, Ibn Battuta decided to visit India and try his luck at the court of the sultan of Delhi, Muhammad Ibn Tughluq. He arrived in 1333, after a grueling and dangerous journey. Then he made his way to the sultan's court, with his train of servants, wives, and gifts of horses, camels, and slaves for the sultan.

Ibn Battuta was well received by Muhammad and appointed to the office of judge. In his book, *The Travels*, he describes Delhi as "a vast and magnificent city, uniting beauty with strength" and the sultan as "of all men the fondest of making gifts and of shedding blood." In 1354, Ibn Battuta returned to Morocco and dictated his account of his travels. He died in 1369 at the age of 64.

South India through the Eyes of Travelers

The two great independent kingdoms of South India—the Hindu kingdom of Vijayanagar and the Muslim Bahmani kingdom

In the 13th and 14th centuries, southern India was raided many times by the Khalji and Tughluq sultans of Delhi. Their attempts to subdue the south were unsuccessful and led, in the middle of the 14th century, to the formation of two independent southern kingdoms—the Muslim Bahmani kingdom and the Hindu kingdom of Vijayanagar. The dividing line between the two was the Krishna River, and the history of both kingdoms is dominated by their long-running battles over this fertile area.

Camel caravans were the usual form of transport for goods throughout India.

Athanasius Nikitin

Athanasius Nikitin set off from his home in Russia on a commercial visit to India in 1468. He spent four years at the rival Muslim-ruled Bahmani capital of Bidar. He was the only European to have visited it at that time. He describes it as the chief city of Muslim India but comments on the contrast between rich and poor Bahmanis: "People... in the country are very miserable, while the nobles are very **opulent** and delight in luxury." He says the nobles were carried from place to place "on their silver bed," accompanied by horsemen, foot soldiers, and musicians. Nikitin died before he could return to Russia. Fortunately, his account of his travels and experiences was carried safely to Moscow by some merchants in 1475.

What the Merchants Saw in Vijayanagar

The Hindu kingdom of Vijayanagar ruled over the far south of India for more than 200 years. It was founded in 1336 by two brothers, Harihara and Bukka, and reached its peak under King Krishna Deva Raya, who ruled from 1509 to 1530. He further expanded the kingdom and encouraged lucrative trade with Portuguese merchants and travelers. Gold, silver, horses, and Ceylonese elephants were imported into Vijayanagar. Rice, sandalwood, cloves, and dyes were the major exports. Many of the Portuguese visitors commented on Vijayanagar's splendor and prosperity. Its huge citadel was surrounded by rings of fortifications and guarded by a large army. It had beautiful palaces, lavishly decorated temples, and wide streets. Duarte Barbosa wrote in 1518, "Among the most prized of the royal possessions are the elephants and horses, the king usually possessing more than nine hundred elephants and twenty thousand horses." The king himself was described by a Portuguese traveler as "the most feared and perfect king that could possibly be, cheerful... and very merry. He is a great ruler and a man of much justice."

The End of the Empire

By the middle of the 16th century Vijayanagar's power had begun to decline. The Hindu kingdom had resisted the Muslims but, in 1565, it was defeated by neighboring Muslim sultans at the battle of Talikota. Much of the city that had been described by the Portuguese traveler Castantheda in 1552 as "the greatest known to the whole world" was destroyed.

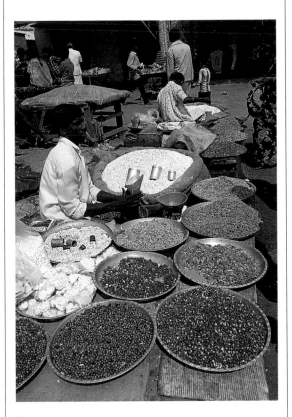

This modern-day street vendor in Mysore (South India) is trading in a market virtually unchanged since the 14th century. The snacks he is selling give some idea of the variety of food that has always been eaten in India

Nicolo de' Conti

The Italian Nicolo de' Conti visited Vijayanagar in the early 15th century. He reports that the city was 60 miles around and had a population of at least 90,000. He also writes that the king had 12,000 wives "of whom 4,000 follow him on foot wherever he goes" and "a like number... ride on horseback." The rest were carried in **litters**. De' Conti witnessed some of the many wars between the Bahmani and Vijayanagar. He also describes the rite of sati where a Hindu wife is required to throw herself on her dead husband's **funeral pyre** (sati was banned in 1829). De' Conti began his travels to Asia in 1419. He did not return to his home in Venice until 25 years later, in 1444.

The modern-day ruins of Vijayanagar at Hampi

The Mogul Empire

The extent of Mogul power by about 1605

The first Great Mogul, Babur

During the 16th century, much of India came under the control of another group of Muslims from the north-west—the mighty Moguls. They succeeded in establishing one of the most powerful and splendid empires ever seen, famous for the grandeur of their courts, buildings, gardens, art, and literature. They were also famous for their six strongest rulers, known as the Great Moguls. These rulers started to explore India in detail and devised brilliant systems of communication and administration in order to rule. When the British came along 200 years later they took over many of the Mogul systems of government.

Babur

The first Great Mogul, and the founder of the dynasty, was Babur, who ruled from 1526 to 1530. In 1526, Babur marched from his capital in Kabul, Afghanistan, into India and defeated the last sultan of Delhi, Ibrahim, at the battle of Panipat (see page 21). This gave him control of Delhi and Agra, which became the twin capitals of his empire. Babur was a fantastic general. By the time he reached India, he had fought against Turkish, Afghan, and Persian forces. He studied his enemies' tactics and formed them into one highly successful strategy. Even his greatest efforts, however, were no match for the Hindu Rajput warriors who defeated him in 1527.

Humayun

Babur's son, Humayun, was unable to defeat the Afghan forces of Sher Shah. In 1540, Humayun fled to Persia, but the Moguls later defeated the Afghans and Humayun returned to India in 1555. Unfortunately, he died in 1556 before he could win back all of his lost lands.

Akbar the Great

The greatest Mogul emperor of all ruled a court that was larger and richer than that of Elizabeth I of England (who ruled at the same time as he did). Akbar was the grandson of Babur and came to the throne at the age of 14. Akbar's reign lasted for 49 years, from 1556 to 1605. He strengthened the empire and reconquered the lands lost by his father. Akbar also won back the loyalty of the nobles. Just as importantly, he gained the allegiance of the powerful Rajputs by marrying a Rajput princess.

Akbar realized that the Muslim Moguls could only rule India successfully if they involved the Hindus and other non-Muslims. He banned the hated tax imposed on non-Muslims and on Hindu pilgrims and employed many Hindus in his administration.

The magnificent fort in Agra dates from the 16th and 17th centuries, when Agra was the capital of India.

Akbar loved riding and playing polo. He was a skilled swordsman and a good shot.

Fatehpur Sikri

In 1570, work began on the building of Akbar's new capital city, Fatehpur Sikri, to the west of Agra. Legend says that it was here that a Muslim holy man, Shaikh Salim Chisti, foretold the birth of Akbar's three sons. The prophecy came true. Filled with gratitude, Akbar had a beautiful sandstone city built and moved his court from Agra. But Fatehpur Sikri was abandoned after just 14 years, probably because of problems with the water supply. Many of its amazing buildings still survive, including Shaikh Salim Chisti's tomb.

Two views of Fatehpur Sikri today and a painting from Akbar's Memoirs showing the city being built

A *Mogul painting of a Jesuit priest*

What the Jesuits Saw

Among the Christians who visited Akbar's court were **Jesuit** missionaries from the Portuguese colony at Goa. Three Jesuit fathers arrived at Fatehpur Sikri in February 1580 and were welcomed. Akbar even built them a chapel inside his palace. The Jesuits were disappointed, however, in their attempts to convert Akbar to Christianity. Other Jesuits followed. In their accounts, they describe Akbar as a man of "medium stature, and strongly built. He wore a turban on his head, and the fabric of his costume was interwoven with gold thread.... On his brow he wore several rows of pearls or precious stones."

A young Mogul prince visiting some Hindu monks as part of Akbar's policy of religious tolerance

Exploring India's Religions

Akbar had a deep interest in religion. He summoned Muslim, Hindu, **Parsi**, Jain, Christian, and Jewish scholars to his court and spent many hours talking to them about their religious beliefs. Akbar amassed a large library of religious books of all types. In 1582, he announced the formation of his own new religion, the Din-i-Ilahi, or Religion of God. Akbar brought together the best from all the religions he had studied.

Akbar died in October 1605. Like his father and grandfather, he left a detailed history of his life, the *Akbar-nama*, recorded by his **chronicler**, Abul Fazl.

Akbar's hardest campaigns were against the Hindu Rajputs. He captured the great Rajput fortress of Chittorgarh (below) in Rajasthan in 1568. He later formed an invaluable alliance with the Rajputs.

Jahangir embracing Shah Abbas of Persia (c.1620)

Jahangir

Jahangir followed his father, Akbar, on to the Mogul throne and reigned from 1605 to 1627. The 17th century was the golden age of the Moguls. They had luxurious palaces built, sat on jewel-encrusted thrones, and surrounded themselves with finery. European visitors to the Mogul court were greatly impressed by its wealth and spectacle.

Jahangir followed his father's policies of treating both Muslims and Hindus with equal respect. Jahangir loved art and nature. His memoirs include many descriptions of unusual birds and animals illustrated by court painters. He had a reputation for cruelty and drunkenness, as well as for gentleness and charm.

In 1611, Jahangir married Nur Jahan, the "Light of the World." She became one of the main sources of power behind the throne, raising her family and her favorite, Shah Jahan, to high positions in the court. When Jahangir died in 1627, Shah Jahan was crowned emperor.

Sir Thomas Roe (1581–1644)

Thomas Roe at Jahangir's Court

England's first ambassador to India, Sir Thomas Roe, spent four years at Jahangir's court, from 1615 to 1619. He had been sent by King James I to seek a trade treaty from the emperor. He wrote an account of his life at the court and his experiences of Jahangir himself. Among many other details, he describes the strange ceremony that took place on the emperor's birthday. Jahangir sat on a set of golden scales and was weighed against sacks of gold and precious stones. These were later distributed among the people.

Jahangir weighing his son Prince Khurram (later Shah Jahan) against gold on his birthday in 1607. From The Memoirs of Jahangir, *c.1615*

A *Mogul painting of Shah Jahan and his wife Mumtaz Mahal*

Shah Jahan

Shah Jahan reigned from 1627 to 1658. He is best remembered for the great buildings that he commissioned, such as the Red Fort in Delhi, the Agra Fort, and, of course, the Taj Mahal (see page 31). This was built as a memorial for Shah Jahan's wife Mumtaz Mahal, the "Chosen One of the Palace," whom he married in 1612. Her sudden death in 1631, after the birth of her 14th child, left Shah Jahan devastated with grief. He spent two years in mourning.

After Mumtaz Mahal's death, Shah Jahan left the business of wars and campaigns to his sons and devoted himself to his great passion for architecture. He also loved jewels and gemstones. His throne was the famous and fabulous "Peacock Throne." The canopy over the throne was held up by 12 emerald pillars. At the top of the pillars were two peacocks standing on either side of a tree, inlaid with rubies, emeralds, pearls, and diamonds.

In 1658, Shah Jahan fell ill. His third son, Aurangzeb, killed his older brothers, imprisoned his father in Agra Fort, and declared himself emperor. Shah Jahan died in 1666.

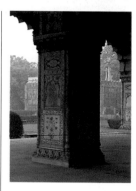

The Red Fort in Delhi was begun by Shah Jahan in 1638 and finished some ten years later. The fort is built from massive blocks of red sandstone.

Aurangzeb receiving the head of one of his brothers, his main rivals to the throne, on a plate. When Aurangzeb came to Shah Jahan's throne, he called himself Alamgir—"World Conqueror."

Aurangzeb

Under Aurangzeb, the last of the Great Moguls, the Mogul Empire reached its greatest size. But Aurangzeb's reign also heralded the beginning of the end for the Moguls. Aurangzeb ignored Akbar's policy of **religious tolerance** and equality. His narrow-minded belief in Islam lost him people's trust and resulted in many rebellions against his rule, including those by the Sikhs (see page 35), the Rajputs, and the Marathas (see page 35). Aurangzeb reintroduced the tax on non-Muslims and ruthlessly destroyed many Hindu temples, often building **mosques** on top of the ruins.

Aurangzeb died in 1707. Soon afterward the Mogul Empire began to disintegrate, weakened by invasions and infighting. There were emperors in place until 1857, but they ruled in name only. In 1858, the British sent the last emperor, the King of Delhi, into exile.

The Taj Mahal

The *Taj Mahal stands on the west bank of the Yamuna River near Agra. Shah Jahan summoned architects and craftsmen from all over the Mogul Empire and beyond to build this tomb for Mumtaz Mahal. He wanted it to be the most beautiful building ever created. Various designs were submitted to him and each was tried out as a wooden working model. The final design was probably a mixture of these ideas and Shah Jahan's own ideas. Building began in 1632 and took about 20 years to complete. The Taj Mahal is built of white marble and was originally decorated with precious stones. Inside are the tombs of Mumtaz Mahal and Shah Jahan. Legend has it that Shah Jahan intended building a black marble replica of the Taj Mahal on the opposite bank of the river, as his own tomb, but he was imprisoned by Aurangzeb before he could put his plan into action.*

4 The European Presence in India

European Traders

Portuguese trade routes in the 15th and 16th centuries opened up the way for Europeans to sail to India.

Vasco da Gama was born in 1460 into a military family. Discipline was the hallmark of his leadership. He died in Cochin in 1524.

Dutch trading ships of 1640 (below)

Ocean Exploration

In July 1497, the Portuguese navigator Vasco da Gama led an expedition of four ships and 170 men out of Lisbon harbor at the start of a historic journey. He sailed around the Cape of Good Hope, up the east coast of Africa, and across the Indian Ocean. In May 1498, he reached the port of Calicut on the west coast of India and became the first European to reach India by sea.

*W*ealthy Portuguese traders enjoyed a privileged lifestyle. Here a merchant is being greeted by his Indian household and servants.

Da Gama was given a lukewarm welcome by the Hindu ruler of Calicut, who dismissed the goods he had brought with him as cheap trinkets. The Muslim merchants were not pleased to see the Portuguese, either. Da Gama did manage to load his ships up with precious spices, however. In fact, he made enough profit from his cargo to cover his expedition expenses 30 times over.

More Portuguese Follow

A second Portuguese expedition sailed for India in 1500, led by Pedro Alvares Cabral. Cabral set up a trading post, or "factory," at Cochin. Da Gama led a third expedition in 1502. Both of these expeditions used force to squash any opposition. For the next hundred years, the Portuguese controlled the trade in the Indian Ocean from their base at Goa on the west coast of India.

Trading Wars

Toward the end of the 16th century, Portuguese control of India began to weaken. By the early 1600s, Dutch and British merchants had set up their own rival East India companies to trade in India and Southeast Asia. The Dutch had the upper hand in the spice trade of Southeast Asia. The British, therefore, fixed their sights firmly on India. They set up their first trading post at Surat in 1612. By the late 17th century, their main rivals in India were the French, who had established their own trading company in 1664 and their first trading post at Pondicherry. By 1690, the British had also settled in Madras, Bombay, and Calcutta. Throughout the 18th century, the British and French fought for trading supremacy, with the British finally emerging as the victors.

The English East India Company

The English East India Company was set up in 1600 to trade with India and Southeast Asia. At first, the company was solely concerned with the spice trade. But then the Mogul Emperor Jahangir allowed it to deal in silk, cotton, **indigo**, and so on within certain parts of India as a reward for protecting Muslim pilgrims from Portuguese raiders as they traveled to the holy city of Mecca. These exotic materials quickly became a part of life for wealthy people back in Britain.

As Mogul power weakened (1666–1707), the company seized any opportunity to control India and its trade. The English East India Company eventually formed the basis of the British Raj (rule) in India (see pages 36–41).

*M*ain trading posts

A Dutch plantation in India in the 17th century

European Travelers

The royal burial place in the fortified city of Golconda. Newbery and Fitch visited this place on their way to Fatehpur Sikri and Akbar's court.

An English traveler in India at about the time of Ralph Fitch's journey.

Ralph Fitch

Ralph Fitch traveled to India in 1583 as one of the first group of English merchants to arrive there to trade. The leader of the group was John Newbery. One of Fitch's duties was the delivery of letters from Queen Elizabeth I to the Emperor Akbar. Newbery and Fitch were arrested in the Persian Gulf by the Portuguese and sent to Goa, where they were accused of spying and put in prison. Eventually, they were released on bail and told not to leave Goa. As soon as they could, they fled from the town and escaped. Fitch described the city as "Golden Goa" because of its wealth.

Newbery and Fitch made their way to Akbar's court at Fatehpur Sikri and delivered the letters from the queen. On the way to Fatehpur Sikri, they stopped off in Golconda, a city whose exquisite diamonds were world famous. Fitch and Newbery then went their separate ways—Newbery back to England and Fitch eastward down the Yamuna and Ganges rivers to Bengal. Newbery was never heard of again. Fitch returned to England in 1591.

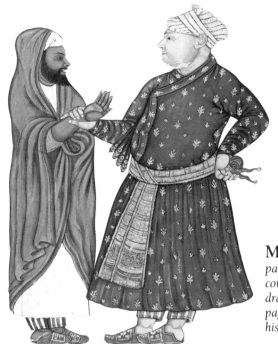

Manucci feeling a patient's pulse. He commissioned this drawing for the front page of the account of his adventures.

Niccolao Manucci

In 1653, aged 14, Niccolao Manucci ran away from his home in Venice to go to sea. He reached Surat in 1656, then made his way to Agra.

At this time, there was a struggle for power going on between Aurangzeb (see page 31) and his eldest brother, Dara. Manucci joined Dara's army as an **artilleryman**. When Dara was defeated at the battle of Samugargh, Manucci fled, donned a disguise, and joined Aurangzeb's army instead. He later joined up with Dara again and rose to the position of captain of artillery. When Dara was killed by Aurangzeb, Manucci left the army and continued his travels to Delhi, Agra, and Bengal.

The Adventures Continue

For the next few years Manucci fought with the Rajputs in the Deccan and made a small fortune (which he lost again) practicing as a doctor, although he had no medical training whatsoever. His lucky break came when he cured one of the royal family of an ear complaint and was appointed official physician. In 1681, however, Manucci left his post and made his way to Goa. His amazing adventures continued. The Portuguese viceroy sent him on a mission to the Marathas and rewarded him with a knighthood for his efforts. He then served the English governor of Madras as correspondent between the English and Aurangzeb. In return, he was given land and a house in Madras. He died there in 1717.

Shivaji and the Marathas

An English doctor, John Fryer, who traveled to Persia and India from 1672 to 1681, wrote about the two most remarkable characters of the time—the Great Mogul Aurangzeb and his deadly rival Shivaji, leader of the Hindu Marathas. Shivaji rose from humble origins to become the symbol of Hindu resistance against Aurangzeb's religious intolerance. He was hero-worshiped because of his exploits in battle and his adventures, such as his escape from Aurangzeb's court. Until his death in 1680, Shivaji tricked and outwitted Aurangzeb. His son, Shambuji, was killed by Aurangzeb in 1689. But Shivaji's spirit lived on. In the early 20th century, his memory was revived to inspire Indians fighting for independence from the British.

A *19th century drawing of Sikh warriors*

Sikh Religion and Resistance

The Sikh religion was founded in the late 15th century by the first guru (teacher), Guru Nanak. It contained elements of Hinduism and Islam. During the 17th century, the Sikhs were persecuted by Aurangzeb and their ninth guru was murdered in 1675 for refusing to convert to Islam. To protect themselves, the Sikhs formed their own army, called the Khalsa. Members of the Khalsa had to wear or carry the five symbols of the Sikh faith. These are the five *ks*—*kes* (uncut hair), *kangha* (a comb), *kirpan* (a dagger), *kara* (a steel bangle), and *kachh* (breeches or shorts). The Khalsa fought bravely against the Moguls, and they succeeded in establishing Sikh rule in the Punjab under Maharaja Ranjit Singh (reigned from 1799 to 1839).

5 The British Raj 1756–1947

Explorers and Rulers

By 1756, Mogul power was at an end. By the end of the century, Maratha power was also over. In their place, the English East India Company had been steadily expanding its strength and influence. The company remained, however, a trading concern, directed by a board and the **shareholders** in London. In 1756 to 1767, all this changed and the English East India Company's attention turned to land and politics. The company even had its own army to protect its interests. The company had an important base in Calcutta, Bengal. In 1756, in an effort to regain power, the nawab (a prince) of Bengal marched into Calcutta and defeated the company's troops. The British retaliated under the leadership of Robert Clive at the battle of Plassey in 1757. The nawab was soundly beaten and the company effectively became the ruler of Bengal. The victories of Clive over the French East India Company from 1745 to 1761 made the English company's hold over India complete. By the early 19th century, it had extended its control over much more of India.

The Battle of Plassey in 1757, where the British Lieutenant-Colonel Robert Clive defeated the anti-British ruler of Bengal, Siraj-ud-Dawlah, consolidating the English East India Company's control over Bengal, the largest province in India.

British India up to 1765.

British India up to 1857.

A European trying to learn Persian from a local teacher, or munshi

The Asiatic Society

In 1784, the Asiatic Society of Bengal was founded by Sir William Jones, a British lawyer, judge, and **linguist**. Its aim was to encourage the study of Indian languages, literature, and culture. Jones had mastered European languages and Turkish, Persian, Arabic, and Hebrew. On his arrival in India, he learned Sanskrit so that he could translate ancient Indian texts into English. Jones's work led to a growing interest in Sanskrit literature in Europe and many other scholars of the language joined the society, such as Thomas Colebrooke (1765-1837) and Dr. Horace Hayman Wilson, who became the first professor of Sanskrit at Oxford University.

The defeat of the Indian forces at Jhansi in 1858

The Rising of 1857

In 1857, resentment that had been building up among Indians against the East India Company and the British came to a head. The army was mostly made up of Indian soldiers, or sepoys. They were issued rifles with cartridges that had to have the tips bitten off before they would fire. Rumors started that the bullets were greased with cow fat (which was unacceptable to Hindus, who consider cows sacred) or pig fat (unacceptable to Muslims, who consider pigs unclean). The sepoys refused to use the bullets and mutinied. The so-called Indian Mutiny, or First War of Independence, quickly spread across North India. The rebellion had no real leaders and eventually fizzled out after two years. A great deal of anger and suspicion remained on both sides for many years to come.

The Crown Raj

The British government had begun to take a closer interest in the way the East India Company ran its affairs in India. The government was not always happy with what it saw and realized that changes needed to be made. In 1858, it was decided that the company should be abolished and the government of India should pass directly into the hands of the British Parliament and Crown. A viceroy (governor) was appointed to represent the Crown in India and a secretary of state for India was appointed in London. In 1876, Queen Victoria was officially proclaimed empress of India (although she never visited India). Until 1947, India was to remain the "brightest jewel in the **imperial** crown."

British officials conducting part of the survey from the safety of their camp

The Great Survey of India

As well as being a time of political expansion, the 19th century was also a time of geographical exploration. The British Survey of India was begun in 1800, with the aim of producing accurate maps of the country. It was not an easy task! The surveyors' equipment was heavy and cumbersome and there were tigers, snakes, dense jungles, and the threat of **malaria** to cope with.

Many of the plants and animals the survey found were shipped back to Britain to be studied at Kew Gardens and London Zoo.

Queen Victoria in 1876, seated on a throne given to her by the raja of Travancore

Maharaja Dulep Singh, painted in the 1850s

Some of the 600 princely states of India. The states were too scattered to form a threat to the British Raj. They were finally recognized by the leaders of independent India in 1971.

JAMMU & KASHMIR

PUNJAB

PATIALA

BAHAWALPUR

BALUCHISTAN BIKANER DELHI

JODHPUR JAIPUR

SIND UDAIPUR GWALIOR

UNITED PROVINCES

BIHAR

REWA

CUTCH BARODA BHOPAL SURGUJA

JUNAGADH INDORE CENTRAL INDIA AGENCY BENGAL

BASTAR

HYDERABAD ORISSA

BOMBAY

KOLHAPUR

MYSORE MADRAS

COCHIN

TRAVANCORE

Princes and Politics

Throughout India's history, its kings and princes have played important and colorful roles. Some leaders were famous for their wisdom and courage in battle, others for their fabulous wealth and the splendor of their courts and lifestyles. Many of their palaces can still be seen in India today, although the princes are now princes in name only.

The Princely States

During the time of British Crown rule, India was divided into two parts. About two-thirds of the country was governed directly by the British. The rest was made up of some 565 Indian "princely" states, ruled by maharajas, rajas, nizams, and so on. These princes were allowed to keep their titles and their lands, in return for swearing allegiance to the British. Some states, such as Hyderabad, were huge and very wealthy; others were tiny, covering less than a square mile in area (see below left).

The beautiful Lake Palace in Udaipur, Rajastan. Built by Maharaja Jagat Singh II in 1754, it is now used as a luxury hotel.

Ranjit Singh, ruler of Punjab

Ranjit Singh— the "Lion of Punjab"

The Sikh kingdom of the Punjab (see map on page 38) was one of the last regions of India to come under British control. Maharaja Ranjit Singh, known as the "Lion of Punjab," ruled his kingdom shrewdly and bravely from 1799 to his death in 1839. Although he was a Sikh, he sought the advice of many Hindus and Muslims who lived in Punjab and managed to maintain religious harmony in his kingdom. The British could not overpower Ranjit Singh. Instead, they were forced to sign treaties of "perpetual friendship" with him. Ranjit Singh was a vital part of British plans to take over Afghanistan and had to be kept on their side. With his help, the British succeeded in getting rid of the strong Afghan king Dost Muhammed and replacing him with a weak ruler, Shah Shuja, who would act on behalf of the British. The result was disastrous, however. The Afghans rebelled and returned Dost Muhammed to his throne.

When Ranjit Singh died, no strong ruler took his place. After two Sikh Wars in 1845–1846 and 1849, the Punjab also came under British control.

British officers being entertained at the court of an Indian prince in 1820

The City Palace in Jaipur, home of the maharajas of Jaipur since the early 18th century

Treasure and Poverty

Many of the larger princely states were famous for their legendary wealth. Some princes lived in great luxury, eating off golden plates and wearing clothes of gold and silver thread. The last nizam of Hyderabad was reported to be one of the world's richest men. There were jewels everywhere in his palace, including emeralds the size of eggs and buckets and buckets of pearls. The royal family of Baroda owned a pearl necklace with pearls as big as marbles and jewelry said to have belonged to **Napoleon Bonaparte**. The maharaja of Jaipur's treasure was so well guarded that the maharaja himself had difficulty in being allowed to see it.

But there was another side to India— that of poverty. The majority of people living in India were very poor due to harsh systems of local taxation and famine. The combination of droughts, floods, and badly **irrigated** land sometimes caused appalling shortages of food.

From finery to famine—victims of the Madras famine in 1878

Life in the Raj

New British arrivals in Bombay in 1916

The heyday of the British Raj from 1858 to 1905 saw a great influx of people from Britain in search of jobs in the government, **civil service**, or army. Many were fairly well-off already; others came to seek their fortunes. They sailed from England on ocean liners, down the Suez Canal to Aden, then across the Indian Ocean. On reaching the Suez Canal, passengers were allowed to change into their "tropical dress." The journey lasted several months, giving them plenty of time to prepare for the culture shock ahead. They also had time to read the many helpful pamphlets available, such as *How to Pack, How to Dress, How to Keep Well on a Winter Tour of India (for Ladies)* and *Notes for Officers Proceeding to India.*

Fanny Bullock Workman dressed for mountain climbing

Women Travelers

Most of the women who went to India rarely traveled, if they could help it. But a few were more adventurous. An American, Fanny Bullock Workman, became famous for her bicycle rides and mountaineering. In 1898, she and her husband biked from Cape Comorin all the way north to Peshawar and the Himalayas. She wrote down details of every building they passed but was much less interested in the people of India. Between 1898 and 1912, she climbed many of the highest Himalayan peaks.

During the Raj, the British had thousands of miles of railroad track laid all over India. This enabled more Indians to travel and make pilgrimages and allowed **nationalist** feelings to be communicated throughout the country. This photograph was taken by Colonel Yule in 1863. British officers were encouraged to take photographs and these proved invaluable aids to scholars, surveyors, the government, and the army.

Hunting and shooting were popular among British officers and Indian princes alike.

Arrival in India

In India itself, British society was divided into a rigid order. At the top of the scale came the senior government officials and civil servants; below them came army officers, then businesspeople, then ordinary soldiers, and then Indians. In the 17th and 18th centuries, employees of the East India Company had often married Indian women, but by the 19th century, this was frowned upon. Most British people kept themselves separate from the Indians, apart from upper-class Indians such as the princes. Many considered the Indians to be inferior to them. Most of the British felt they had a duty to rule India, but not to get involved with the people or culture of the country.

Business as Usual

Many British people in India tried to carry on their lives pretty much as they would have at home. They brought their servants, furniture, heavy clothes (often unsuitable for a hot climate), and even pets with them. They had English food and wine sent over from home. Once in India, they surrounded themselves with households of Indian servants—cooks, fan-pullers, ayahs (nannies), and so on. While their husbands were out at work, the women had plenty of time on their hands. They painted, wrote letters home, went to church, and organized balls, garden parties, and amateur dramatics to fill their days. Among the men, polo, hunting, badminton, and going to their clubs were favorite leisure activities. In the hot season, people escaped to the cool of the hill stations, such as Simla in Himachal Pradesh.

A Christian missionary in India

Missionary Fever

In 1813, the ban on British missionaries traveling to India and settling there was lifted, although the British still weren't keen on missionaries until the 1830s to 1840s. A wave of missionaries set sail in the hope of converting India's "benighted **heathens**" to Christianity. Despite their best efforts, very few Indians became Christians. Quite a large number of the converts were low-caste Hindus or poor Muslims who looked to Christianity as a means of escape. There were some notable pioneer British missionaries such as William Carey, who translated the Bible into Indian languages, and Alexander Duff, who shaped the educational system of India through missionary schools for the working classes.

6 Modern India

Toward Independence

Toward the end of the 19th century, a new, nationalist reform movement began to take hold in India. It was led by a group of young, wealthy, educated Indians who believed that Indians should be in charge of their own country and that it was time for the British to go.

The Indian National Congress and Muslim League

The Indian National Congress was founded in 1885 as a political party dedicated to getting the views of Indians heard in government. Gradually, self-rule for India became its aim. Among its founders and first presidents were Mahadev G. Ranade (1842–1901) and Gopal K. Gokhale (1866–1915). Both taught that it was time for India to reform and stand on its own two feet. They were joined by the more radical Bal G. Tilak (1856–1920), who believed that India needed to be free first before it tackled reform.

Congress was a mainly Hindu movement and, in 1906, the all-India Muslim League was founded by Aga Khan. The league was initially a pro-British organization, but with the election of Mohammed Ali Jinnah to its leadership, home-rule, and eventually the establishment of the state of Pakistan, became its aim.

An all-India Muslim League rally demanding a separate Muslim state within or apart from India

Mahatma Gandhi with Sarojini Naidu, the first Indian woman to be elected president of congress, in 1925

Mahatma Gandhi

One of the most important and influential figures in the Indian independence movement was a lawyer, Mohandas K. Gandhi (1869–1948). Gandhi spent 20 years in South Africa, where he worked to try to lessen the discrimination shown toward Indians. He returned to India in 1915. Gandhi worked with the congress but he also spread the message of independence to the mass of India's population by visiting thousands of countryside villages over a period of many years. He became known as "Mahatma," which means "Great Soul."

The British failed to keep their promises of a greater share of power for Indians and they also ignored the contribution made by Indians who fought in World War I. The final straw came in 1919 when the British massacred 400 Indians at **Jallianwala Bagh**. Gandhi urged people to follow his policy of nonviolent, passive resistance. He also encouraged them to stop buying British-made cloth and to spin their own instead.

Independence and Partition

In his book, The Discovery of India, Nehru explored his own ideas of what sort of country India was and how it might develop.

After World War II, it became obvious that the British could not justify their presence in India for very much longer. The Quit India campaign gained momentum. In 1947, the British government appointed Lord Mountbatten as the viceroy who would preside over India's independence. India became an independent country on August 15, 1947, with Jawaharlal Nehru, Gandhi's greatest follower, as its first prime minister. But there was a price to pay for freedom. The all-India Muslim League had been campaigning for a separate Muslim country, Pakistan, which would include part of Punjab in the west and Bengal in the east. Millions of people were forced to leave their homes and millions more were killed in the violence that followed. This is known as the partition of India. Gandhi also became a victim of the Hindu-Muslim rivalry. In January 1948, he was shot dead by a Hindu fanatic who resented his concern for the Muslims. Nehru remained as prime minister until his death in 1964.

Lord Mountbatten, India's last viceroy, being greeted by people shortly after the announcement of India's independence

Hindu-Muslim rivalry erupted in violence and rioting in the major Indian cities. These were the scenes in the streets of Bombay in 1946.

A map showing the partition of India

Technological achievements include solar power plants and an advanced space program.

A cooking pot shop in Jaipur, Rajasthan

The countryside in Goa

Traditional crafts

India Today

India has made great strides forward since becoming an independent country in 1947. It is the biggest democracy in the world, playing an important part in Asian and world affairs as a member of the **Commonwealth of Nations**, the Nonaligned Movement (for countries that are not closely linked with either the United States or Russia), and the United Nations. India's industries have grown rapidly during nearly 50 years of economic plans and it is a major producer of iron, steel, and coal. Its cotton and silk textiles are still in demand, as they have been for thousands of years. Agricultural production has increased rapidly but has been overtaken by the demand for food. But India remains a country of great contrasts, with the traditional existing alongside the modern. There are hundreds of small handicraft industries all over India, producing papier-mâché work, wood carving, brass ornaments, tie-dye, **batik**, and mirror-work.

Facing the Future

One of the main problems facing India in the future is its ever-increasing population. By the year 2000, it is estimated that there will be more than 950 million people in India, putting a great strain on the country's land and food resources. It is very difficult for the government of India to cope with the increasing population in cities. People are being encouraged to have smaller families. Legislation is soon to be passed that will limit members of Parliament to two children or less to set an example!

Problems still remain among some of the different religious groups in India. India and Pakistan are still in conflict over the future of Kashmir, one of the old group of princely states (see pages 38–39). There are Sikh calls for their own independent country, Khalistan, in the Punjab. In 1984, the prime minister of India, Indira Gandhi, Nehru's daughter, was assassinated by her Sikh bodyguards. There have been violent clashes between Hindus and Muslims, most recently over a disputed holy site in Ayodhya.

The Calcutta Stock Exchange

Handmade pottery being sold in the street

Indian children

The New Explorers

Despite its problems, India continues to exert its magic and fascination over people. In the 1960s, the new invaders were hippies from Europe who came to India in search of spiritual enlightenment! Today, thousands of tourists visit India to explore its sights and the glories of its checkered past—the Taj Mahal of the Moguls, the palaces of the rajas and maharajas, and the Victorian stately homes of the British. Alongside these are the particularly Indian sights, sounds, smells, and experiences that have lasted through thousands of years of visitors, invaders, and explorers.

The elephant-headed Hindu god, Ganesha

Blue houses in Jodhpur, Rajasthan

Modern-day India covers some 1,274,000 square miles and is divided into 26 states and several **union territories**. About 850 million people live in India, making it the second most populous country in the world, next to China. Hindi, English, and 13 regional languages, together with hundreds of local languages and dialects, are spoken in India.

India	Europe	Other
c.5000 B.C. Farming has begun in western parts of India.	c.6500 B.C. Farming begins in Greece and spreads to other areas of Europe.	9000 B.C. Hunters spread throughout North and South America.
c.2500 The Indus Valley civilization is at its height.	c.3000 Use of copper spreads throughout Europe.	c.2500 The horse is domesticated in central Asia.
c.1500 The Aryans invade from the north-west. Their Vedic religion forms the basis of Hinduism.	c.1600 Mycenaean civilization begins in Greece.	c.1500 The use of iron begins in Turkey. c.1200 The Jewish religion emerges.
326 Alexander III of Macedon (Greece) crosses the Indus River into India.	510 The Roman Republic is founded.	c.650 Iron is being used in China. c.230 The Great Wall of China is built.
A.D. 50 Trade flourishes between India and the Roman Empire.	A.D. 43 The Roman Empire invades Britain.	A.D. 30 Death of Jesus Christ. Spread of Christianity begins.
c.320–550 The Gupta Empire and the golden age of Hinduism in India.	117 The Roman Empire is at its greatest extent.	300s The Ghanaian Empire is founded in West Africa.
630–645 The Chinese Buddhist monk Hsuan Tsang visits India.	262 Bubonic plague spreads through Rome.	622 Muhammad founds the religion of Islam in Arabia.
1001 Mahmud of Ghazni begins a series of raids into North India.	959 The Unification of England.	935 The text of the Koran finished. 960 Sung dynasty in China.
1206 The Delhi Sultanate is established in North India.	1066 The Normans conquer England.	c.1000 The Vikings colonize Greenland and travel to America.
1336 The rise of Vijayanagar. 1347 The rise of Bahmani.	1340s Black Death, a form of bubonic plague, spreads throughout Europe.	1352 Ibn Battuta travels to Africa. 1368 Ming dynasty in China.
1498 The Portuguese (led by Vasco da Gama) arrive in India.	1492 The first globe is made in Germany by Martin Behaim.	1492 Christopher Columbus reaches the Americas.
1526 The founding of the Mogul Empire in India.	1532 John Calvin starts the Protestant movement in France.	1530s The European slave trade begins across the Atlantic Ocean.
1619 The English East India Company sets up its first factory, at Surat.	1618 The Thirty Years War of religion starts.	1607 The first English settlement is founded in America (Virginia).
1632 Shah Jahan begins building the Taj Mahal, in memory of his wife.	1667 The French begin to expand under Louis XIV.	1644 Manchu dynasty in China. 1680 Rozvi Empire in Zimbabwe.
1720 The French establish a trading post at Pondicherry near Madras.	1707 England and Scotland unite.	1699 The French establish the colony of Louisiana in America.
1784 The India Act. The British take political control of India.	1756 The Seven Years War begins. c.1760 The Age of Enlightenment.	c.1700s The European exploration of Africa begins.
1799–1839 Ranjit Singh rules over the Sikh kingdom of Punjab.	1789 The French Revolution begins.	1775 The American Revolution begins.
1857 The First War of Independence (also called the Indian Mutiny).	1807 The slave trade is abolished in Britain.	1789 George Washington becomes the first president of the United States.
1876 Queen Victoria is proclaimed empress of India.	1884–1885 The Conference of Berlin (Germany).	1861 The American Civil War begins.
1920 Mahatma Gandhi launches his campaign of civil disobedience.	1914–1918 World War I.	1917 The U.S. enters World War I.
1947 India gains independence. 1948 Gandhi is assassinated.	1939–1945 World War II.	1941 The U.S. enters World War II.
1962 India-Pakistan wars. 1964 Jawaharlal Nehru, India's first prime minister, dies.	1961 The Berlin Wall is built in Germany.	1961 John F. Kennedy becomes U.S. president. 1963 John F. Kennedy is assassinated.
1966 Nehru's daughter, Indira Gandhi, becomes prime minister. 1971 India-Pakistan War.	1972 The European Community gains more members.	1965–1973 The U.S. is involved in the Vietnam War.
1984 Mrs. Indira Gandhi is assassinated. Her son, Rajiv, takes over.	1985 Mikhail Gorbachev becomes the leader of the Soviet Union.	1981 Ronald Reagan becomes the U.S. president.
1991 During an election campaign, Rajiv Gandhi is assassinated. 1991 June, P. V. Narasimha Rao elected prime minister.	1989 Boris Yeltsin becomes leader of Russia. 1991 East and West Germany are united. The Berlin Wall is destroyed.	1993 Bill Clinton becomes the U.S. president.

Glossary

A

archaeologist: a person who studies the past by methodically **excavating** ancient sites and **artifacts**.

artifact: an ancient object.

artilleryman: a soldier who operates guns and cannon.

B

banyan: a tropical tree whose roots grow above ground before they reach down into the soil.

bartering: goods that are exchanged for other goods are bartered.

batik: a way of making a pattern on cloth with wax. The wax design is applied to the cloth, which is then dipped in dye.

C

chronicler: someone who writes down an account of a person's life.

citadel: a fortress, often built on top of a hill overlooking a city.

civil service: the administrative staff who carry out the orders of the government.

Commonwealth of Nations: an organization of states that were once (or still are) ruled by Great Britain.

D

delta: the area at the mouth of a large river where the river meets the sea and drops its load of sediment.

deported: exiled, banished, or sent away from a country.

dialogue: a piece of writing in the form of a conversation.

Durga: a warriorlike Hindu goddess shown riding on a tiger and carrying various weapons in her ten arms.

E

enlightened: to have seen the light, or the truth of the matter.

envoy: a messenger or representative of a king or queen.

excavated: dug up in a methodical and scientific manner.

F

funeral pyre: a large pile of wood on which a dead body is cremated (burned).

H

heathen: the name given by followers of some religions to people who do not share their particular beliefs.

I

imperial: when one country politically or economically dominates another (or many countries), it is described as imperialist.

indigo: a dye made from vegetable matter that has a violet-blue color.

Indo-European: the people and group of languages that originally came from the region between and including India and Europe.

irrigate: to water an area of land by a system of canals or waterways.

J

Jallianwala Bagh: a massacre of Indians by the British army on April 13, 1919, in Amritsar. The army opened fire on people who had illegally assembled for a Hindu festival in a walled garden.

Jesuit: a member of the Roman Catholic Society of Jesus, founded by St. Ignatius in the 16th century A.D.

K

Kublai Khan: (c.1215–1294), ruler of China and Mongolia, and grandson of Genghis Khan.

L

linguist: someone who speaks or writes a variety of languages.

litter: a chair carried by servants.

M

malaria: a disease spread by mosquitoes in tropical Asia and Africa. Symptoms include high fever, then severe chills. Malaria can be fatal and can recur.

Mesopotamia: the area between the Euphrates and Tigris rivers (modern-day Iraq). In Mesopotamia, the civilizations of Sumer and Babylon thrived.

middlemen: merchants who buy goods from the producer and then sell the same goods on to the trader who will in turn sell them to the consumer.

missionary: someone who tries to convert people from one religion to another.

monsoon: seasonal winds that occur in Asia. They blow from the southwest in summer bringing heavy rains, and from the northeast in winter.

mosque: a place of worship for Muslims.

muslin: a very fine cloth made out of cotton that looks like gauze.

N

Napoleon Bonaparte: (1769–1821), a general who made himself the French emperor after his success in the French revolutionary wars.

nationalist: someone who is devoted to his or her country and believes in its independence.

O

Old Silk Road: the route or routes used by merchants carrying silk westward from China.

opulent: very rich or wealthy.

orientalist: one who studies the cultures and languages of the East.

P

Parsi: a follower of Zoroastrianism, a religion that spread from Iran to India in the seventh century A.D.

patronage: financial support and encouragement given by someone such as a king to favored artists.

pilgrimage: a journey, made as an act of religious devotion, to a sacred place.

proclamation: a public announcement made about important affairs of state.

R

reincarnation: the belief that, when you die, you are reborn into another life.

relic: anything that once belonged to a saint or religious figure.

religious tolerance: recognition and acceptance of other people's beliefs.

republic: an independent country that has no monarch and is ruled by an elected government.

revival: a renewal of interest in something such as art or literature.

S

Sanskrit: the ancient language of India, which has special importance as the sacred language of the Hindu holy books.

shareholders: people who own shares in a company. A share is a certain percentage of the wealth of the company. The company is expected to generate profits to increase the investment that the shareholder has made.

T

tortoiseshell: the shell of sea turtles.

U

union territory: a region, such as a large island or city, that is part of India but does not count as a separate state.

Index

Numbers in **bold** indicate an illustration. Words in **bold** are in the glossary on page 47.

Afghanistan **4**, **6**, 8, 20, 21, **22**, **26**, 39, **45**
Agra **4**, **26**, **27**, 28, 30, 31, 35, **38**
Akbar the Great **27**, 28–29, 31, 34
Alexander of Macedonia **10**–11, 46
all-India Muslim League 42, 43
Arabs 19, 20, 23
archaeology 7, 47
art **11**, 14, **15**, 26, 29, 47
Aryans 5, **8–9**, 46
astronomy 15
Aurangzeb 30–**31**, 35

Babur **26**, 27
Bahmani **24**, 25, 46
Bangladesh **4**, **45**
battles 8, **10**, 12, 24, 25, 26, 35, 36, 38
British 5, 7, **15**, 26, 31, 33, **34**, 35, 36–**37**, 38, **39**, **40–41**, 42, **43**, 45, 46
British Raj 33, 36–**37**, 38, **39**, **40–41**, 46
Buddhism 5, **11**, 12, **13**, 14, **15**, **16**, 17, 46

caste system 9, 13, 41
cave paintings **15**
China 16–**17**, 18, **22**, 23, **45**, 46, 47
Christians 11, **28**, **41**, 46, 47
civil disobedience (non-violent resistance) 42, 46
Classical Age of India 14–15
Clive, Robert **36**
cotton 5, 15, 18, 33, 44, 47
Cunningham, Sir Alexander **7**

da Gama, Vasco **32–33**, 46
de' Conti, Nicolo 25
Delhi **4**, **6**, 16, 20, 21, **22**, **23**, 24, **26**, 30, 35, **36**, **38**, 46
dharma 12
dialects 45
Din-i-Ilahi (Religion of God) 29

East India companies 33, 36, 37, 41, 46
empires 10, 11, 12–13,
14–15, 16, 18, 19, 21, 26–27, 37, 46
Europeans 5, **23**, 24, 29, **32–33**, **34–35**, 36, 45, 46
explorers 5, 16–**17**, 20–21, **22–23**, 24, 25, 26, **34–35**, 37, **40**, 45

Fa Hsien 16–17
famine **39**
farming 7, 8, 44, 46
Fatehpur Sikri **4**, **26**, **28**, 34
Fitch, Ralph 34
five "ks," the 35

Gandhi, Indira 44, 46
Gandhi, Mahatma **42**, 43, 46
Ganges River **4**, **8**, **12**, **13**, **13**, 17, 20, **26**, 34, **45**
Ganges Valley 8, 14, 21
Goa **4**, **18**, 23, **26**, 28, **32**, 33, 34, 35, **44**, **45**
gods 5, **9**, 11, **14**, 17, **45**
Golconda **2**, **4**, 34
Greeks 10–11
Gupta kings 14–15, 16, 46

Harappa **6**, 7
Himalayas **4**, **8**, **16**, **22**, 40, **45**
Hinduism 5, 9, **14**, 16, 19, 20, 21, 24, 25, 26, 27, **29**, 31, 33, 35, 37, 39, 41, 42, **43**, 44, 45, 46, 47
Hindu Kush **4**, **8**, 10, **16**, **22**, **26**
Hsuan Tsang **17**, 46
Humayun **26**
Huns, the 15

Ibn Battuta 22, **23**, 46
independence 21, 35, 37, 42–43, 44, 46, 47
Indian Mutiny 37, 46
Indian National Congress 42
Indus River **4**, **6**, 7, **8**, **10**–11, **12**, **14**, **16**, 19, **26**, **45**, 46
industries 44
Indus Valley Civilization 5, **6–7**, 46
Islam 5, 19, 20, 23, 31, 35, 46

Jahangir **29**, 30, 33
Jainism 29
jewelry 7, 20, 39

Khalsa, the 35
kingdoms 8, 13, 14, 15, **19**, **24**, 25, 38, 39, 46
Krishna River **4**, **12**, **14**, **24**, **26**, **45**

languages 5, 13, 14, 19, 36, 41, 45, 47
literature 14, 17, 19, 26, 36

Mahabharata 8
Mahal, Mumtaz **30**, 31
Mahmud of Gazni 20, 46
Manucci, Niccolao **35**
Marathas, the 31, 35, 36
mathematics 15
Maurya, Ashoka 12–13, 14
Maurya, Chandragupta 11, 12
Mauryan Empire 11, 12–13, 14
merchants 7, 18, **19**, 22, 24, 25, 33, 34, 47
Mesopotamia 6, 47
missionaries 16, 28, **41**, 47
Mogul Empire 21, **26**–27, 28–29, 30–31, 33, 36, 46
Moguls 5, 35, 45
Mohenjo Daro **4**, **6–7**
monsoon winds 4, **18**, **19**, 47
Muslims 5, 19, **20–21**, 22, 23, 24, 25, **26**, **27**, 28, 29, 31, 33, 37, 39, 41, 43, 46, 47

Nehru, Jawaharlal **43**, 44, 46
Nikitin, Athanasius 24
Nonaligned movement, the 44
numerals 15

Pakistan **4**, 5, 6, 8, 42, **43**, 44, **45**, 46
Parsi 29, 47
partition of India **43**
Persia **10**, **22**, 26, **29**
Polo, Marco **22**
population 44, 45
Portuguese 23, 25, 28, **32–33**, 34, 35, 46
poverty 5, 24, 39, 41
princely states of India **38**, 39, 44
Punjab **4**, 10, 35, **36**, **38**, 43, 44, **45**, 46

Queen Elizabeth I of England 27, 34
Qutb ud-Din Aibak 20–21

Rajputs 26, 27, **29**, 31, 35
Raziya (Sultana) 21
Red Fort **30**
religion 5, 6, 7, 9, 12, 13, 14, 16, 19, 29, 31, 35, 39, 44, 46, 47
Rig-Veda, the 9
Roe, Sir Thomas 30

Romans 11, 18, 19, 46

Sanskrit 9, 13, 14, 16, 17, 19, 36, 47
sati 25
science 14, 15
Shah Jahan 29, **30**, 31, 46
Shivaji 35
Sikhism 5, 31, **35**, 39, 44, 46
Singh, Ranjit—the Lion of Punjab **35**, **39**, 46
Slave Dynasty 21, 47
spices 5, 18, 19, 33
sultans 20–21, 23, 24, 25, 26, 46

Taj Mahal, the 5, 30, **31**, 45, 46
Timur 21
trade 7, 8, 14, 22, 23, **25**, 30, 34, 36, 46
traders 5, 11, 18–19, 23, **32–33**, 47
travelers—see explorers
tribes **3**, 4, 5, 8, 15

United Nations, the 44

Vijayanagar **24**, 25, 46

wealth 5, 18, 20, 23, 24, 25, 27, 29, 33, 34, 38, 39, 42, 47